Praise for *Evelyn As*

Christine Butterworth-McDermott's *Evelyn As* is a vivid, poetic account of the early life and career of late 19th and early 20th Century chorus girl, artists' model, and actress Evelyn Nesbit. These dynamic, fraught, and textural poems provide a stunning and heartbreaking portrait of a life of stardom, violence, scandal, and survival, weaving together everything from the Persephone myth and Little Red Riding Hood to Rapunzel and Snow White—not to mention also gaze theory, the sometimes (wildly complicated) transformative power of art, and the roles we all play both willingly and un-. At its heart, *Evelyn As* is a compelling, gripping, and tragic blockbuster of a book, simultaneously cinematic, awe inspiring, and crushing.
—Matt Hart

"We like to say, that in spring, you rose," Christine Butterworth-McDermott writes of Evelyn Nesbit, "from a city of coal and ash / American-made, transformed… our girl our dream." With the utmost care in these nimble, transformative verses, Butterworth-McDermott offers us a vision of the American project through the (unfortunately timely, and fortunately timeless) reinvention of a woman so voraciously consumed, dissected by the public. But Butterworth-McDermott's vision of Nesbit in these all-consuming poems is one of constant and important reinvention, of both self and society. Butterworth-McDermott places herself— and us! — alongside Nesbit so that together they can realize we are capable of rising from the ash because "all things resurface," and we should "take satisfaction in the knowledge."
–D. Gilson

In these poems, Butterworth-McDermott undoes the red velvet cloaks, rolls up the bear rugs, and dismantles the swings that made the child model, Evelyn Nesbit, famous. We see past the blinding lights of Stanford White's photography bulbs to Evelyn as a young girl trapped in a system of nightmarish power. Telling her story through the lens of famous figures

that include Persephone, Little Red Riding Hood, and Scheherazade, Evelyn As connects a long line of nightmarish narratives together. In the process, Butterworth-McDermott's poems slash through centuries of female objectification.
—Julie Babcock

Evelyn As is a timely and timeless tale told by a speaker who weaves myth and fairytale to retrace the many forked paths of Nesbit's life. This collection offers a moving apology to a girl who lost her girlhood to the overindulgence of many adults around her. In portrait after portrait, Butterworth-McDermott documents Nesbit's early life in searing detail, moving the poet's sympathy and ire and her desire to unwind the past. As she writes in the book's incantatory final line: "may everything done be undone."
–Jen McClanaghan

Evelyn As

*Portraits of Evelyn Nesbit
December 25, 1884 – June 25, 1906*

Christine Butterworth-McDermott

Fomite
Burlington, VT

Copyright © 2019   Christine Butterworth-McDermott

All rights reserved. No part of this book may be reproduced in any form or by any means without the prior written consent, except in the case of brief quotations used in reviews and certain other noncommercial uses permitted by copyright law. This is a work of fiction.

ISBN-13: 978-1-944388-73-7
Library of Congress Control Number: 2018961891
Fomite
58 Peru Street
Burlington, VT 05401

*for all the Evelyns
and for Brett*

Contents

Evelyn As Model	1
Evelyn as Exhibition in Twenty-Four Pictures: A Guide	2

Portraits of Evelyn Nesbit, with White 1884-1901

Evelyn As Persephone: An Anticipation	13
Evelyn As Cinderella: In the City of Ash, 1900	17
Evelyn As Little Red with Velvet Swing	18
Evelyn As Geisha Girl	24

Portraits of Evelyn Nesbit, almost Barrymore, almost Thaw

Evelyn As Quivering Pink Poppy	31
Evelyn As Little Red, with Second Wolf	38
Evelyn As Patient	43
Evelyn As Rapunzel Without Hair	45
Evelyn As Princess, Longing to Be Rescued	46
Evelyn As Le Bébé	47
Evelyn As Ghost	50
Evelyn As Rapunzel In Her Tower	53
Evelyn As Small Animal	55
Evelyn As Prisoner	56
Evelyn As Escapee	59

Portraits of Evelyn Nesbit, Adrift, 1904-1905

Evelyn As Persephone: Out of the Underworld	63
Evelyn As Reflection	65
Evelyn As Snow White	66
Evelyn As Automata	68
Evelyn As Alice	69
Evelyn As St. Maria Goretti	70
Evelyn As Beauty	71
Evelyn As A Collapsed Flower	72

Portraits of Evelyn Nesbit Thaw, Pittsburgh 1905

    Evelyn As Fashionable Bride   77
    Evelyn As Cinderella: In the Palace of the Prince   79
    Evelyn As Greeted by the Christian Friends of Mother Thaw   81
    Evelyn As Scheherazade   83
    Evelyn As Mediator   84
    Evelyn As Bodily Parts   85

Portraits of Evelyn Nesbit Thaw, New York, June 1906

    Evelyn As Tourist Of Her Own Past   91
    Evelyn As Life and Death   93
    Evelyn As One of Millions   97
    Evelyn As Lost Child   98
    Evelyn As Witness   99
    Evelyn As Out of Body Experience   101
    Evelyn As The Center of a Broken Pomegranate   102

    Evelyn As Elegy   104

Notes   *107*

"And he told me again that he was my friend, that he always would take care of me, that he always would see that no harm ever came to me, that he wanted me to tell him the whole thing, and that he would not think any the less of me if I told it to him, and he wanted me to tell him the whole thing, he said. So I began by telling him how and where I had first met Stanford White."
   —Evelyn Nesbit-Thaw's testimony at her
   husband's murder trial, 1907

"The tragedy wasn't that Stanford White died, but that I lived."
   —Evelyn Nesbit, 1934

Evelyn As Model

It's complicated
               the way, at only fourteen,
     you gaze out

of the frame of Käsebier's photograph

child-woman.
half-inviting us in:

girls like you,
have always been labeled

angel   (whore   vixen)   victim
kittens   pet   snake

I see how you clutch the pitcher,
as if you hope to shatter

the china, break the flash
                                light
of the camera trained
on you.

Your gaze speaks sadness –
but that may be just the way I see it

since I'm not looking to be seduced

Evelyn as Exhibition in Twenty-Four Pictures: A Guide

1. Evelyn Florence McKenzie & Winfield Nesbit, *Florence Evelyn Nesbit—Beginning Sketch*, 25 Dec, 1884. Tarentum, Pennsylvania.

   It may be apocrypha that the child was so beautiful at birth, the neighbors came to gaze in awe. Her father, enchanted by his girl, read her fairytales and called her his star, a child of flashing light. He was dead by the time she was eleven.

2. Evelyn Florence McKenzie, *Florence Evelyn—Charmer* (1893). Pencil sketch. Pittsburgh, Pennsylvania.

   Evelyn, shown as a penniless girl, a Cinderella, who must mend the financial woes of her mother. Pretty girls learn to collect payment from boarders any way they know how. It is not known what Evelyn learned from the male clientele.

3. Evelyn Florence Nesbit, *First Pose at Fabric Counter* (1898). Philadelphia, Pennsylvania

   Mrs. Nesbit worked at a fabric counter, that employed adolescent Evelyn. An artist spied the auburn-haired beauty folding linen. Eventually, several other reputable artisans paid her a dollar (approximately thirty dollars in modern equivalency) per hour to sit. Five hour stints of immobility earned her letters of introduction, used when the family moved to New York City.

4. James Carroll Beckwith, *Portrait of Evelyn Nesbit* (1901), oil on canvas, 78.7 × 67.3 cm, Private collection.

    Mrs. Nesbit failed as a seamstress but her daughter's face was a success and Evelyn supported her family by modeling. James Carroll Beckwith painted the topless fourteen-year-old, a dark kimono just slipping from her shoulders.

5. John C. Fisher Co., *Evelyn as Floradora Girl* (1901). Photographic print.

    Evelyn joined *Floradora*, a revue of dancing showgirls; Mrs. Nesbit agreed to this occupation because "*Floradora* girls marry millionaires." Evelyn was so popular she was promoted to the role of Spanish maiden.

6. Anonymous. Evelyn Nesbit in Broadway's *Wild Rose* (1901). Photograph. New York City, New York.

    Newspapers ran the headline, "Her Winsome Face To Be Seen Only from 8 to 11 p.m." In the audience were three men who would become intimate with Evelyn: Stanford White, John "Jack" Barrymore, Harry Kendall Thaw.

7. Morceau Studio. *Portrait of Stanford White—Well Known Member of the firm McKim, Mead and White* (1906). Photograph. New York City, New York.

    Stanford White, a year before his death at fifty-two (five years after his affair with Evelyn), was the premier architect of the United States. His firm was responsible for the wide popularity of the Beaux-Arts style. Many of their designs in New York City and Newport, Rhode Island still stand today. Less respectably, the married White had multiple clandestine liaisons with chorus girls. Though she nicknamed him "Stanny Claus," he affectionately called her "Kittens," and showered her with gifts—wind-up toys, satin kimonos, jewelry, clothes, fox furs, etc.— he also drugged and raped Evelyn when she was only fifteen.

8. **Charles Dana Gibson, *The Eternal Question*, (1905), pen and ink.**

Evelyn was one of Charles Dana Gibson's favorite models, and posed for him several times in the early 1900s. Here, her hair is arranged as a question mark, signifying the secrets of femininity.

9. **Gertrude Käsebier, *Miss N.*, (c. 1898), print 1902, Platinum Print, 7 7/8 in. x 5 9/16 in.**

Evelyn leans forward, looking directly out of the photograph, wearing a loose white gown that shows both shoulders. Her dark hair is drawn up in the Gibson girl style and she holds a delicate cream pitcher. Much has been made of the duality of her sexuality and innocence in this particular photograph.

10. **Rudolf Eickemeyer, *In my studio or Tired Butterfly* (1901), Photographic print. Gelatin.**

Mrs. Nesbit left Evelyn in the care of White and went on a trip to Pennsylvania. White promised "his pet" he would have her portrait taken by the city's best photographers, including Rudolf Eickemeyer. Eickemeyer and White provided direction and costuming, posing Evelyn as Little Red Riding Hood, a Turkish maiden, in a blonde Gainsborough wig, with a crown of yellow chrysanthemums, and on a bearskin rug. Hours later, exhausted, she fell asleep. Eickemeyer struck by her vulnerable figure in the lush black kimono snapped his most famous photo.

11. FAO Schwarz, West 24th St. (1899). Museum of the City of New York. Archival print.

Above the famous toy store, White had a secret loft where he met young showgirls. Nondescript outside, the inside was, in the words of Nesbit, filled with velvet that was "a wonderful red." Hanging from the ceiling was a swing on red velvet ropes. White found it arousing to have the girls swing upwards to puncture large Japanese parasols with their bare feet. Often it was more than their feet that were bare. Also in the apartment was a bedroom, entirely paneled with mirrors.

12. Alfred S. Campbell Art Co., *With Stuffed Tiger Head*, 1902. Archives of American Art. Smithsonian Institution. 1 postcard : ill, 14 x 9 cm.

A typical postcard of Evelyn. She is dressed as a Greek goddess and leans on a tiger's head, above its open mouth. Other postcards show Evelyn holding kittens, sniffing flowers, or in states of reverie or undress.

13. Anonymous. *Pretty Faces Hold Men's Gazes*. Collage, Evelyn Nesbit images. c. 1900-1904. New York City, New York.

Clothed, semi-nude, and nude images from photographs by notable photographers as well as images from *Vanity Fair, Ladies' Home Journal, Woman's Home Companion, Harpers' Bazaar, Cosmopolitan*, Advertisements for toothpaste, face cream, sheet music, beer trays, tobacco, sausage, pocket mirrors, postcards; calendars for Coca-Cola, Prudential Life Insurance, Swift.

14. **Anonymous.** *John "Jack" Barrymore.* c. 1902. New York City, New York.

> Twenty-one-year-old Barrymore was a struggling illustrator at *The New York Evening Journal*. Evelyn and Barrymore met at a party given by White in Madison Square Garden. He was smitten, having seen "Evie" over twelve times in *Wild Rose*. When the young lovers turned serious, Mrs. Nesbit, who felt Barrymore was too poor, and White, who was jealous, shipped Evelyn off to a school for girls. Barrymore pined and left notes around the school but Evelyn did not, or could not, respond. Shortly after, Barrymore began his professional career as an actor.

15. **Advertisement. "Pamlico": The Henry C. de Mille School for Girls (1899). A beautiful home-school in the country. Advantages of New York City. All Departments. Thorough training in sewing, cooking, and house-keeping. Pompton, New Jersey.**

> Stanford paid for Evelyn's stay at this school run by Cecil B. DeMille's mother. While there, Nesbit may have had an "appendectomy" (a euphemism at the time for abortion). During this time, White often visited Evelyn, who grew pale and lost all her hair due to stress. Another attentive visitor, Mr. Harry Kendall Thaw, was quite persuasive in his courtship of the ill eighteen-year-old, promising her a relaxing trip to Europe for her and her mother.

16. **Anonymous.** *Harry Kendall Thaw* (1895). Photograph. 5 x 7 inch. b & w.

> The spoiled scion of a Pittsburgh railroad fortune was noted for his incoherent babbling, random laughing,

baby talk (he dubbed Evelyn "Boofuls"), and temper tantrums. Perhaps in an effort to medicate his mental illness, Thaw injected speedballs (large amounts of cocaine and morphine). Thaw had a penchant for whipping prostitutes and/or hotel help in bathtubs until skin was broken. His domineering mother covered up his wrong-doings with hush money. Initially Thaw tried to court Evelyn under the pseudonym Mr. Munroe, but later revealed himself as Thaw. Although Mrs. Nesbit knew of the rumors regarding her daughter's suitor, she did not tell Evelyn.

17. **Anonymous. Harry Kendall Thaw and Evelyn Nesbit with Evelyn's mother in Paris. Pencil. 3 ¼ x 5 ¾ inch.**

Thaw pressed Evelyn to marry him, but she declined, eventually citing the loss of her virginity. Already obsessed with White, Thaw alternately blamed the "Beast," Evelyn's mother, and Evelyn herself, waking her up at night again and again to confess. Evelyn fought with her mother who had White pay her passage home. Thaw and Evelyn continued to sightsee, pretending to be married. In Domremy, Thaw wrote that Joan of Arc "would not have been a virgin if Stanford White had been around."

18. **Joh. F. Amonn, *Schloss Katzenstein* (c. 1900), 1 korrespondenz-karte: ill, 14 x 9 cm.**

Thaw rented this large German castle, dismissed the staff, and kept Evelyn as prisoner. Over a span of two weeks, he repeatedly whipped and sexually assaulted her. When they returned to traveling, Evelyn met friends of White who helped her book passage back to New York.

19. Evelyn Nesbit, *New Pose, Old Pose* (1904). Pencil sketch. New York City, New York.

In New York, Evelyn and White saw each other again, but he had moved on to other girls. Fearing for her financial stability, and believing her status as a non-virgin ruined her for other men, Evelyn was susceptible when Thaw returned, penitent, laden with gifts, and asking for her forgiveness.

20. Announcement of Marriage. April 5, 1905 *The Saint Paul Globe*. Front page.

Harry Kendall Thaw wed Evelyn, a "former opera singer," on April 4, 1905, with Mrs. Thaw's hesitant approval. Concerned primarily with propriety, Mother Thaw made sure Evelyn's past was not spoken of. Still estranged, Evelyn asked her remarried mother to attend the wedding but this did not renew their relationship.

21. "Lyndhurst" (William & Mary C. Thaw mansion), 1165 Beechwood Boulevarde, Squirrel Hill, Pittsburgh, Pennsylvania (1887-89, demolished c. 1942), Theophilus Parsons Chandler, Jr., architect.

The home in Pittsburgh, where the newlyweds lived with Mother Thaw. After six months of relative calm, Thaw decided to have dentists remove the veneers on Evelyn's teeth, which White had paid for. He also had her pose as Bluebeard's seven wives, a popular, if morbid, trend. At this time, Thaw began an obsessive effort to expose White, going so far as to correspond with Anthony Comstock, urging him to expose White as a sybarite. Convinced White knew of his efforts—he thought White had hired hitmen to kill him—Thaw began carrying a gun.

22. National Art Views, Co., *Café Martin: Fifth Avenue Restaurant* (c. 1905), 1 postcard: photograph, 14 x 9 cm.

Along with *Rector's* and *Sherry's*, this was one of the most popular restaurants at the turn of the century due to its cosmopolitan atmosphere. After convincing Evelyn to go on a European holiday, Thaw traveled with her to New York in late June 1906. On the evening of the 25th, the couple met two friends, Truxton Beale and Tommy McCaleb. Arriving later, Evelyn realized Harry was drunk, and perhaps high on a speedball. Evelyn saw White with his son but ignored him, only revealing she'd seen them after they had left.

23. Anonymous. *Crowd at the Rooftop Theater at Madison Square Garden* (1900). Photograph. Museum of the City of New York.

The night of June 25, 1906, Thaw bought tickets for a new show. It was the first time Evelyn had been there since moving to Pittsburgh. Thaw acted strangely, pacing back and forth. Shortly before the end of the show, the couple and their friends got up to leave. During the chorus of "I Could Love a Million Girls," Thaw turned back to shoot White three times in the head, at close range. Since a bullet entered above the left eye, White's face was destroyed and blackened by gunpowder. When Thaw was arrested, he claimed White deserved it for having "ruined my wife."

24. Cover page, "Harry Thaw Kills Stanford White on Roof Garden" 26 June 1906. *New York American*.

The subsequent trial was the first to be called the "Trial of the Century." Throughout the aftermath, photographers and reporters focused on Evelyn, who was painted as both vixen and victim. She was pursued by the flash of the photographers' cameras for most of the decade.

**Portraits of Evelyn Nesbit,
with White 1884-1901**

Evelyn As Persephone: An Anticipation

New year's eve: 1900

Madison Square Park
           aglow   with three thousand
                               Chinese lanterns

hung by Stanford White

Near Brooklyn Bridge
                fireworks
                        explode
in flashes of light
                        and the century begins
in jubilant dissonance

        in a night so dark
                  it's not black
                          but maroon, like blood,
like the center
                  of a broken pomegranate.

She isn't there yet
                but it's already
                      a beginning.

❧

When Evelyn Nesbit was a child
        she loved
                apples
red as velvet

cake   (*Happy Birthday*)

December 25: Christ's day, her day

>—Mama, does that mean I'm special?
>—Yes, Florence Evelyn, it does.
> You are blessed

    with beauty
that springs eternal.

>(May that old horned goat, Hades,
>never come.)

>On Christmas day, they always sing Ava Maria.
Ava. Eva. Eve. Evelyn.
>(*blessed blessed blessed* remain *blessed*)

                          ※

Seven-year-old Evelyn loves the tales
her father tells her

>about magic potions,
>glass slippers,
>white flowers,
>about red apples,
>about
>   getting lost

>>in the woods

>>*The poor child, who did not know*
>>*that it was dangerous*
>>*to stay and talk to a wolf,*
>>*said to him, "I am going to see*
>>*my grandmother and carry her*
>>*a cake and a little pot*
>>*of butter from my mother."*

Evelyn Evie

                angel-child

        in a white robe   Persephone

                (May you never follow the wolf.
                 May that old horned goat, Hades,
                never come.)

                ❁

After her father dies, she thinks how he called her
    a star, a light   a flash

she thinks perhaps he is watching over her

Later, white flower petals drop on the floor
    in a Pittsburgh boarding house
        one by one by one
her Mama cleans them up, saying,

        —Go collect the rents, Evelyn.
            They'll be persuaded by your face.
        —No, Mama, I don't want to go
            with the nice men.

        Persephone spits pomegranate seeds into a bowl
        watches them float in the bile.

                ❁

Behind the counter in Philadelphia, she folds the fabric,
and at fourteen, she is already

    Gibson's eternal question
        the hair   the gaze   our guilt

her adolescent innocence

      our knowing glances. O, sweet

modern ancient

      Persephone.

An artist sees her standing over satin,
paints a portrait and money made,
her family is saved,
her fortune is her face—

In 1901, she stands in the city, Stanford's city,
      aglow.

He is forty-six when he sees her,
bud of the bud
on stage in *Floradora*.
Flora adorable. Flower,
fresh as a lily, clean
as white sheets

      He waits for her in the wings
      He waits for her in the underworld

Evelyn As Cinderella: In the City of Ash, 1900

We like to say, that in spring, you rose

from a city of coal and ash
American-made, transformed,
made wondrous

>*Ashenputtel finding her prince*
>*the glass shoe to wear*

our girl   our dream
from city of smoke and ash and coal.

From Pittsburgh
         you'll go

and before you know it, you're up in the air

up on the swing of New York

Evelyn As Little Red with Velvet Swing

At fifteen, Evelyn Nesbit
posed for Eickemeyer.

Stanford White gave her a red velvet cloak
and placed a crown of chrysanthemums on her head
      Gold flowers are the symbol of happiness
                            (and grief)

White chrysanthemums are symbolic
      of lamentation.
In Italy, chrysanthemums are symbolic of death.

Pose.   Flash.
                  Light.
Little Butterfly, he calls her, little
egg shape, chrysalis
unbroken, his to break.

She looks at Eickemeyer's camera
and the tiger's mouth looks at the camera
wide, black, a hole she could dive into
as dark as her mama's hair
when she was ten   before the way men looked at her.

Come on, Kittens, Stanford directs,
smile, wink for the camera, wink

Bewitching
                in the fairy light
le bébé, angel-child
                        Come on, Kittens.
          Flash us that
                smile.

She gathers the white flowers to her bosom.

Evelyn Nesbit stares at the window
of FAO Schwarz.
Above is Stanford's secret apartment.

All the toys, all the stuffed animals

There's a new one wrapped for her
each time she comes

wrapped in a bright red ribbon
tin monkey in a red fez scrambles
a tin tree for a bunch of tin bananas

and a toy tiger, open-mouthed, harmless
(ready to bite)

the apple, fruit, pomegranate, knowledge
                   waiting in the wings

There is always red velvet
in the rooms owned by powerful men

       (some construct swings on the ceiling
       and coax you into them)

higher and higher she swings

toward a hanging paper parasol
        printed with chrysanthemums

He asks her to puncture it

                         her beautiful bare feet

he cries,

again and again and again!

when she comes down, it hangs

like a shredded moon

he takes her hand
and she can feel him trembling

༜

The silk sheets are also red

        This man
        could make you
            —You're meant for something bigger
            than this world, baby
            Trust your Stanny
        This man
        could break you

    Persephone can be rescued if she doesn't eat of the fruit

Everything tastes like chocolate-covered cherries.
She is called little bon-bon, ma chérie, and devoured.

Bear skin rug, mouth of the bear open
Four poster bed, canopied
purple, midnight
curtains drawn by a gold cord

The lights change color from amber to rose to blue

Everything decorated like nymphs' palaces
under the sea. It almost feels like drowning

        The mermaid gave up her voice
        for a prince who did not love her.
        That's a story her father told her.

She was always outside looking in.

Evelyn spins in a room of pillows
and blankets (red orange maroon)

like a dancer in *The Arabian Nights*

❃

Persephone ate half the fruit Hades offered.

> *Drink this, eat this*
> It's labeled
> > *Drink me, eat me*

Here, love, lie down
lie down in this room of mirrors

The walls and ceilings covered

The floor an imitation
glass so seamless it is like a solid sheet of ice

and there she is over and over and over and over;
her small red mouth in an "o."

Flash
            light

Light shatters   refracts in all that reflection

And just for a minute in the reflection of a reflection
she sees the wolf
his teeth
coming at her

> *All the better to eat you with, my dear.*

And there is no huntsman.
And there is no mother.

And there is no father watching over.

She drinks from the bottle that says drink me
There's a buzzing a drumming
        a thump-thump-thumping in her ears
dizzy and sick and everything blurs
and Stanny's voice at a distance
far far away.

❦

And she wakes up in all that velvet
on his bed, his man hands all over her body

And she wakes up and they had been taking pictures of her
sleeping, "The Sleeping Butterfly"

                      waiting in the wings
Flash
        light

into the tiger's mouth, the teeth so bright, so white

Pretend he's not a wolf, *Little Red, pretend, pretend, pretend*

Big game heads on the walls,
rug on the floor
They used to be alive
before they were captured
hollowed out

And she wakes up to blood between her legs, on her hands
His naked manhood against her thigh
A pink undergarment the only costume left.

The blood makes her scream.

For God's sake, don't! He clamps his hand
down over her mouth and she thinks

this is horrible, horrible
and she knows without understanding
how this could be
how this could be

        —Don't cry, Kittens. You belong to me.

※

The incisors of kittens are small
they can't devour and they can't wound.

There is no Father.
There is no God.
There is no huntsman.

No one can save Little Red
as she goes down
in the wolf's arms.

Evelyn As Geisha Girl

Stanford gives you a black kimono to cover yourself.
The Four Gentlemen

    How many gentlemen have been in your life?

in Chinese art refer to:
    the orchid,
    the bamboo,
    the plum blossom
    and the chrysanthemum

    Spring, summer, winter, autumn
        Grief. Lamentation. Death
all over this fine fabric.

    In Eickemeyer's studio, you lied down, to sleep, to dream
    Who knew you would wake up to this

When Stanford told McKim that your mother left you in his care
(of course, in his care), he gasped and said, "My God!"

    —No, Mama, I don't want to go with the nice man.
    —Evelyn, he has your best interests at heart.

    Hades threw Persephone upon his back
    and took her down through sod and stone.

        Persephone, the narcissus
        falls from your breast.

The white petals of you, flayed open

Flash
        light

over and over again

sleeping, sleeping again, and you are sleeping beauty,
you are sleeping, butterfly

And there's pain and there's nothing
It was only a pain, a pain between your legs

In your stomach
little butterflies

                            You remember you drank
                            You remember you ate
                            half of the fruit he offered.

You remember he told you
            of the Chinese lanterns
                    hanging from the trees,
You weren't there,
                  but you imagined it looked
                        like a fairy tale.
                            beautiful,
            you could have cupped one in your hand

    like a blossom,
                orange-red

red as the room
as you remember it
as he created it:
the mirrored ceiling
the velvet swing
tiger's head rug

Tiger skin
stripes seared like marks from a hot grate

You, on striped fur, stripped
down, on all fours in your bloomers

and what did he give you,
                              (it tasted like apples)

and you went down in the dark, a girl
came up to be given a black kimono

against blackness, no one can see
the stains, the drops of blood between your legs.

You can't see blood against black,
and a mouth is a hole as black as a gun
blasting through

And a mouth belongs to the tiger you pose on
And a mouth belongs to a wolf devouring you

You learn to smile into the mouth
of the beast and let him take you

          You're his nice bit, Nesbit
He wraps you in white fox fur
in silk
in orchids and blossoms and chrysanthemums

                    You are covered by Stanny Claus.

Your benevolent father.
Your benevolent vampire.

Flash
                    light
but you were framed

in the room, asleep, drugged,
framed in the bed
the sheets spilling over the edge
the white edge of your gown
stained red

     —Do whatever the nice man wants, Evelyn.
     —Even this, Mama, even this?

Someone later said you are a soft petal torn from a flower.
   If only they knew
     how you'd been pressed between his pages

that inside is blackness
      and the fat red tongue, like velvet, is rough

If only they knew
how he said:
     —Lay back on this pillow, Evelyn.
     —Lay back and rest your weary eyes.

      (—My, what big eyes you have.
      —All the better to see you with, my dear.)

It could have been a fairy tale, a dream,
It was a fairy tale, a dream—
how did it turn
how did it blacken
how did it blacken how did it blacken how did it blacken
how did it blacken to nightmare?

Portraits of Evelyn Nesbit,
almost Barrymore, almost Thaw
1902-1903

Evelyn As Quivering Pink Poppy

Stanford hung three thousand Chinese lanterns
that glowed like chrysanthemums in Central Park.

Stanford hung the moon.
The whole city he designed said so.

Now the autumn sunrise lights up the city of New York.
It glows like a pink poppy—
                  pink and open, like the inside
                  of a split pomegranate.

      O, Evelyn,
                you Persephone,
                          your time
                in this daylit world is short
                for Hades calls

                (and Demeter's protection
                is no where to be found.)

Oh, Evelyn,
what pose do you take? what shape do you make
this time? For what season, for what god?

Stanford had his eye on you from the moment
he hypnotized you with drugs
and led you to bed.

                            ❦

Jack Barrymore had seen *Wild Rose* twelve times before
                he went backstage to meet you.

In your delicate hand, you wrote your phone number
                          on his frayed shirt cuff

For a moment before you let go, you held his wrist,
felt his heart beat there beneath the gossamer of skin,
blue veins underneath, swirling like the patterns
on fine china, white as moon.

And the tabloids read:
      Bohemian Barrymore
            courts Broadway Beauty.

❦

Oh, Evelyn,
     dear sleeping beauty,
    Oh, Sleeping Butterfly,

           Hades posed you there,
            asleep on the dark rug,
naked girl, wrapped in kimono,
               if only Morpheus might let you dream,

    against the flash
                and lights

        Can you ever tunnel from the dark?

O, Evelyn, you pause, mid-pose,

wilting like a flower—arrayed in narcissus, poppy,
                chrysanthemum
    at the door to the underworld.

under the glare of so many lights
that dazzle you, blind you

you've forgotten why you ever
loved this city. It makes you dizzy

in its October darkness; orange
and red like fire and seeds. It gapes

before you like the mouth of a cave
like the mouth of a bearskin rug
ready to swallow you whole

※

Crossing Broadway, you are tired
of all these men who have "your best
interests at heart." Their mouths
wide open with all those teeth

> *All the better to eat you with, my dear.*

and inside is blackness.

      You wonder how many wolves
surround you, how many sniff about

your perfumed body
straight white teeth
your red lips, your dark hair
curling from your head

all of you glowing
like a flowering question mark

※

Stanny comes bearing a pair
of tiny pearls, which he insists
you put in your ears.

Come nearer, he says—

Oh, Evie, this is what he says
    seducer, siren   *snake*

        This is how he makes you feel
        as if you wanted this,
        as if love is impossible,
        without contracts,
        without this terrible payment.

❈

You and Jack spin through
the restaurant—*Rector's*—door
and drink pink champagne
on Stanny's tab

He holds your hand, caresses your wrist.
He says, *you are like a quivering*
pink poppy in a golden
windswept space as if he recognizes you

You want to forget
everything but the pathway lit by Jack's eyes

        but there are pink poppies
        on a gold kimono
                you unfold the material
        Stanny's handwriting
curls away on the kraft paper
which cuts your tender thumb

Your mother says:
        —Don't marry a pauper like that Barrymore.
        Go with the nice man, Evelyn.

You fold up the kimono, like shroud or parasol,
something you'd put high
        on a shelf in the closet.

After all, Jack loves you now

❋

Jack loves you, oh he loves you, and he spins you and he loves you and you and he and yes, oh, yes, you want to say yes and you stay up way past when you should and you miss the chime and everyone thinks you've let him do what no one knows Stanny did and no one knows you fell asleep innocently side by side and all you ever did was kiss

❋

Stanford calls your mother and they wait your return
dawn breaks into the apartment
                        pink and open, like the inside
                        of a split pomegranate

when you and Jack enter hand and hand,
Stanny asks what you will live on

Jack says
    —On love!
but you know how fickle love is
and how love destroys
how lack of love ruins everything

      Look how Stanny smiles as you realize this

     this sugar Daddy's dead
this Daddy's been gone for awhile

You wish you no longer owed him blood.

❋

Blooming love
        is cut off at the root—
You're off to a girls' school
chosen by Stanny and your mama

away from Jack
                —You'll forget him, Evelyn, really
                —Be nice and go away from the good man.

And the tabloids read:
        Miss Evelyn Nesbit will be leaving
        the production of *Tommy Rot*
        to pursue her studies
        and mind her Mama.
                (and the man who buys you everything
                who gives you the seeds
                to destroy yourself)

The inside of a pomegranate
split on the ground

                white petals of narcissus
                red petals of poppies

                      red and white rot in Hades' kingdom

❀

In your dreams, you spin once more through the glass squirrel wheel of Rector's door and everyone at their tables drinking champagne turns to look   at your   snow white   cotton candy spun sugar   beauty   So many gazes and so many faces and so many mirrors   and your red mouth in all the reflections   and your hair   black waves that snake over and over   and everyone is always looking at you.

❋

At Miss de Mille's School for Young Ladies,
they gossip about the man with the moustache.

They gossip about the baubles you return with.
(He likes it when they call him Stanny Claus.)

They gossip about the way he speaks to you,
the way he speaks to them.

You watch, silent, as his eyes blink over their bodies.
You feel buried alive.

                Poppies symbolize resurrection,
        but you are not a poppy
        and there is no wind-swept space

❋

A crushed Jack pins poems and letters
to trees and bushes on the school grounds
they hang unread on the trees until they become
small shredded moons.

Evelyn As Little Red, with Second Wolf

In your dream you are back
in the restaurant, and everyone is looking
at you—you and you and you—in the mirrors
        glass so seamless, a solid sheet of ice
and there you are over
                  and over and over and over,
    your small red mouth in an "o."

Flash
        Light

the light shatters—refracts—
and you see the wolf
        his teeth
coming at you

        Right there during high tea,
        he falls to his knees and puts the hem
        of your beautiful gown, the one Stanny
        bought, to his lips as if he can taste
        your spun-sugar

then you realize this is a memory,
a tall man, smiling
            —I'm an admirer, he says. I'm Mr. Munroe.

The wolf asks you where you live
and you don't tell because you're
a good girl, Little Red,
and you've learned to traverse this path
set by men.

        (O, Evelyn, how could no one tell you
            you took a wrong turn)

Evelyn, if I could travel back to tell you, I would say
        no precautions are enough,
                you have no map for this path.

        The aliased Mr. Munroe saw *Wild Rose* forty times,
        before he had you followed
        by private detectives
        to and from the theater.

O, Evelyn,
O, Little Red, let me speak frankly,

                he, too, had been waiting
      in the wings.
           sending flowers, following you home,
           standing outside your apartment,

and no one told you.

           (—She's going off to school. We can keep it quiet,
              —Why bother her, he's a playboy, he's a child.)

Evelyn, my warning from this distance has no value
Evelyn, my rage has nowhere to go.

Evelyn, they call girls stupid,
        but do not tell them what stalks them
          nor in which guise they come.

※

His name was not Mr. Munroe

        You won't know until later about the bathtub,
        his obsessions with white porcelain

        the feeling of joy
        droplets of blood brought him

       pushing from innocent skin

His roses came wrapped in dollar bills
and even when you sent them back,
your mother kept the money,   *hush.*

       O, Evelyn, let me speak frankly,
your own mother did not tell you
       she recognized him from Pittsburgh,
          city of ash, city of the past.

He rose from the floor and shouted,
"I'm Harry K. Thaw of Pittsburgh!"
as if this would bring everyone,
       to their knees.

And though you yawned, and stretched, and gazed
       over Thaw's head, toward the door
          for someone else to arrive
             Jack, Stanford
       the door did not spin

❀

Later, you will hear how Thaw threw
a party once:
       He invited twenty girls and Sousa
played and jewelry dripped from the glasses
       like bubbles of champagne.
Couples danced round the tables,
       eating pears.

Later, you will hear that, as a child,
Harry danced like St. Vitus
       jerked
          uncontrollably
said horrible things
       face, arms, legs

        twitching
as if he were some puppet pulled by
              an untrained master
and so his whole life he craved control
      and when he could not achieve it,

      he perverted it because no one
in handcuffs can strike you down.

Later, you will hear how when he found
the clerk rude,
      Harry ran through the shop
with his auto
and the glass   shattered
      on the sidewalk
      and inside the store,
on the clerk, who bled
and Harry laughed with joy
at the   red
and laughed
      and laughed
          and laughed
      and laughed
he couldn't stop
      laughing

      ❁

O, Evelyn, why did no one sees fit to tell you?
      No mother. No other chorus
          girl?
O, Evelyn, I would have told you
if you were my daughter or sister or friend
      or the maid at a hotel.
O, Evelyn, I would have begged you
to look for the wolves on your way down the path.

Velvet is pretty and a man over forty is hard to resist
and a man worth forty million is hard to turn away—

Especially for a girl trying
to get out of trouble,
          Especially for a girl
   framed in the room,
    framed on a bed
Especially for a girl
doubling over, doubling down
     stomach searing—

Especially for a girl who must have an appendectomy

     (by which I mean abortion)

Especially for a girl with a shredded moon
for a heart,   crumpling at the foot
   of the bed frame,
       a collapsed poppy.

Evelyn As Patient

It's hard to abort
        a visit when Harry smiles and smiles
and smiles and pays and smiles.

                —Be nice, Evelyn,
                it's just an injection.

                      —Harry's bought the second best surgeon
            in the entire country
                just for you

                to cut you open
to examine your insides, to remove
what's unnecessary.

                    —Listen to your Mama, yes?
                    —Don't strain against me, Evelyn.
                        Be a good girl.
                        Be silent.

                    ❧

Harry holds your hand when you close your eyes
        and there is sleeping
        and there is a sense of floating.

        Your body is just a ship
        to be broken apart
        in the storm and rebuilt

and you open your eyes and Stanny is there,
        eyes wet, holding your hand
                in both of his

                              —Oh, Kittens

and then he rolls away
                    like a ball,
                              out the door
                                        back to his wife
                                        back to his life
                                                  the others
                                        and the up and down
                                                  of the swing

and you open your eyes and Jack is there,
          eyes wet, holding your hand
                    in both of his
                              —Oh, Evie

and then he rises up
                    like a moon,
                              into the sky
                              back to life
                                        and his family
                                        and the stage
                                                  and the curtain
                                                  comes down.

❦

They say they removed / the appendix / but she feels / as if something else is gone / and all / she can / remember / is his blue eyes / wet with tears / and the shredded moons / of love notes / and she doesn't want / to care / anymore / she doesn't want / to love / him / she doesn't want / to love / anyone / oh, Papa / why did you / go away / *our father / who art / in Heaven* / and she is / so tired / her Mama / standing over / her smiling / and Harry is smiling / everyone / is smiling / Harry says / all she needs / is a little vacation / a little rest / she just needs / to be quiet / say yes / come / little Red / little star / precious / go with / the nice man / there's a little boat / near a little / hotel / in a little / French town.

Evelyn As Rapunzel Without Hair

After surgery, Rapunzel,
                all your hair falls out from the morphine

falls out in clumps, falls to the floor
pick up the black petals, curls

like question marks, the eternal questions:
                What is youth?
                What is death?
                What is beauty but something transitory
                                              ephemeral

                        Flash
                                          Light

Your body open and divested
It's all broken
                open in an instant

Blood on your hands

in a basin
on a tablecloth.

Evelyn As Princess, Longing to Be Rescued

Evelyn's answer to Harry Kendall Thaw's marriage
proposal was no.

But she consented to a little vacation
        to see Paris
                and all its lights

What could be so wrong with someone offering
such beautiful little things

                        (poison is poison is poison)

like human hair wigs for her shorn head
        so blonde
               so new
                      and a few dresses, too

and just a little vacation in a little
French town, perhaps a little
au pain instead of more pain
and just a little

                of Thaw, he'll merely follow
                          at a good distance,
                  like a good fairy
              good Harry

Maybe the prayers can be answered.
Maybe the princess can be rescued.

Evelyn As Le Bébé

She floats on a ship,
                angel-child,
away from New York
toward another city of light
away from rotting fruit.

                Did it taste like apples?

Aboard, she thinks of spring
and *The Demeter* in that novel:

      all the dead men, plucked off, sucked
      dry one by one
      like used seeds of a pomegranate
      devoured
      by a vampire.

No one informs her
that the beast is not behind her.

Neighbor Wolf is
the boy next door
      jaws open slobbering dancing dancing an erratic jig

The hound escapes and howls.

❦

Le bébé! Le bébé!, the French journalists shout
and Harry is proud,
                preens like a peacock

Behind him, Mrs. Nesbit's hate is as electric

as a tramway. Evelyn can feel its turquoise glow

      She hates how they fawn all over her
daughter, her youth and beauty,
how they write about her—innocent, pure—
      as if she were some Snow White,
how they unWhite her.

And suddenly, in the glow of that hate,
Evelyn realizes
        —Go with the nice man
was about how much easier
      it would be if she were completely gone
and the attention could rest
        on her mother.

      Feed you to the wolves, my darling.

As they stroll and cool themselves by the water
Mrs. Nesbit complains about
          the heat, the language
But Evelyn loves how no one here understands
      anything about her
except she is le bébé,
        blank and clean and new.

Here, there are no other men but Harry,
      boyfaceround
        and so solicitious, so sweet.

After croissants / near the Bois / de Boulogne / Evelyn goes / back to the hotel / and is cruel / to her mother / lays blame / at her feet / lays the crushed / white petals / on the boarding / house floor / lays the velvet / of the swing / on her shoes / Evelyn explains / how she was / le bébé / and then / was no more / an abandoned child / in the woods / mama / left her / to starve / on her own / mama / let her slide / down the rabbithole / no one / ever / forever / recovers / from that / come / morning / Mrs. Nesbit sails / to London / on White's dime / Evelyn looks /into the deep / pool of water / that is the ocean / with no tears / her mother / says / by way of departure / someday, you'll learn / the errors / of your ways / beggars / can't be choosers / not even / the pretty ones / she gives / a single white / handkerchief / Evelyn picks it / up from the floor / like a flower petal / and crumples it / into her pocket / she is left / bereft / on another continent / once again / chaperoned /only / by an unsprung beast.

※

Evelyn believed Harry
      when he said the bellboy
            rifled through the money
and things got out of hand
            and he threw
him to the floor out of anger

No one informed her how
      his money thawed
out the police concern

that the boy was dragged
            into the bathtub
whipped until
      the blood broke
through the fine skin
and splattered the porcelain
     because that's the way
Harry liked it

No one told her why he spirited her
out of France.

Evelyn As Ghost

You and Harry cross the channel
to look at the tombs of virgins,
at the holy cathedrals,
their stained glass windows with fair angels

              —Angel-child, Harry whispers
as he fingers your gloved palm.

You snap your hand shut like a clam.
              —Bootiful baby, Boofuls, he coos.

You used to have wings,
     You could pose
        flash
              light
as angel or butterfly
as girl or geisha

You hate being grounded

Harry asks again to marry you. You refuse.

He whines, *why not? Don't you love me?*
Is it because of Stanford White?
What did that beast do to you, Evelyn?

            What did he do?
            What did he do?
            What did he do?

Let me be your huntsman. You will dress
in white for me, little beauty, and forget
all that red velvet.

His voice, strange, pleading. He paces
the room, making figure eights over and over.

And no one else has ever cared, not like this.

A prince is not a father.
A prince is not a master.
You whisper your story in the candlelight.

(And this will be the biggest mistake of your life.)

When you reach the climax
          (framed in a room, framed on a bed
          laid down for White on satin sheets,
          appletaste in your mouth)

Harry collapses to the floor
and weeps for you,
face in hands, pawing at his cheeks

        —Poor child! Poor child! Poor child!

It has been so long since someone cried for you,
tears flow for you too and you hold your stomach
afraid the stitches might burst.

It was your mother's fault
          (Did he say Evelyn or Eve, Alice or Persephone?)
that you fell down that damn hole
where she left you to the slime
of caterpillars

Negligent, he says,
full of self-serving neglect

        and you know this is true
        just as you know it's true
        she was a broken woman.

Did she know anything, Evelyn, he asks,
about your maidenly downfall

        —Go with the nice man, Evelyn

at the hands and hooves
of a satyr
like White?

                                    (May that old horned goat, Hades,
                                    never come.)

      Flash
            light

There is a storm in the distance.

Demeter is guilty
        (but Hades is still Hades)
does she deserve
to be vilified
sucked dry

Harry reaches out
to your head and you think
he might yank off the wig
he's given you, strip you
of all that false
blondeness, but instead
he strokes it, back and forth,
strokes everything he's purchased.

      The sun rises like an orange in Paris.

Harry gets up and prowls the room, circling,
circling, and as if he cannot believe it, he asks

you to tell it again and again and again

all night until he is spent
and you are hollowed out.

A ghost of a girl.

Evelyn As Rapunzel In Her Tower

Harry tells Evelyn she needs a change of venue and she whirls
through Europe like whirling
        through the circular doors of Rector's.

She does not know this
        will be a reckoning. They rush
        through the continent.

Harry does not tell Evelyn he had rented the castle
                at Schloss-Katzenstein
for three weeks
        (and dismissed the staff)

She had hoped for a place with an enchanted garden
but everything touched by her small white hands
seems gray as stone.

This Rapunzel, in the tower of her grief, gazes into a mirror.

This Rapunzel, in an actual tower, wonders who could ever love
something so plucked? Who could ever love something so fetal?

This Rapunzel wonders (O, le bébé) how her mother could have
done what she did. This Rapunzel, in her tower
        within a tower, realizes

the tower is the prisonhouse for the body
the body is a prisonhouse for the spirit

This Rapunzel lays her wig over a chair, a headless wonder
        of cascading curls.
She feels her bare head—egg shape, chrysalis

This Rapunzel succumbs to dreams of butterflies,
        pink kimonos, and chrysanthemums.
White chrysanthemums are a sign of suffering.

She dreams of a prince who loved her once.
She dreams of a prince who called her a pink poppy.
She dreams of a prince who almost climbed hair.

This Rapunzel wakes in the moonlight.
        to see her hair at Harry's feet,
He stands upon it—her scalp is his rug.

He is naked.
He is erect.
He has a whip.

He says she is complicit
for going up in the swing
going up and up and there was something
like flying in it
                Flash   light

There is a storm in the distance

He says she must have liked the attention
              all those photographs

                flash flash flash flash flash flash flash flash flash

                The slick whip glows in the moonlight
                as it is raised again and again

She must have wanted
all this

Evelyn As Small Animal

Kittens, your claws are small, they can't
protect, and they can't wound.

His mad face comes down,
He bites your shoulder.

Even as you curl into yourself, a flower
bud upon the bed,
he breaks you open, a flood
of strikes on your back, your breasts, your thighs.

His fingers pry you open—

> Persephone, you are
> nothing but
> a broken pomegranate

Blood splatters
white fabric.

> (O, Evelyn, you poor child)

Evelyn As Prisoner

When Harry retreats, he locks Evelyn in.
She is left for hours to stare
out the window and imagine
                the orange lights of a thousand
lanterns hanging in a park far away

        (how did it blacken to nightmare?)

when she was young. Once upon a time,
life was a fairy tale for a girl
she never got to be.

❃

She runs her hands down
her naked body, tracing where
the strikes hit.

Every morning, in the quiet light,
Harry anoints her with salve.

Later, she picks at the scabs
and watches the blood rise to the surface—

If she gets out who will she tell?
        (not the mama that left her to be locked in)
                Evelyn, Eve, Eva, Ava Maria

If she ever gets out can she ever be
        pure to any father ever again?
                —Oh, Christ, why have you forsaken me?

His dilated eyes did not see her.

For two weeks, she'll wonder
what instruments he'll return with to break

her apart, her body
      criss crossed
the whelp of the welt

      ※

Evelyn wakes again and again in the dark
  (no one can see what happens
   in the dark) For a moment she fears

Harry looming in the moonlight
crop in hand, his words tumbling
like stones and glass, about to bring
down blow after blow
on her snow white skin
cutting it open

but it is only fog through the curtain

and then Evelyn cries into the pillow,
longs for that other room
and all of that soft velvet

Stanny would put her on his shoulders and jog
her around the room, queen
of all she surveyed. Stanny would lay her
down on that tiger skin
so much more gently than this.

      (poison is poison is poison)

She knows there is no father.
There is no mother.
There is no huntsman
and there is no prince.

     Nothing but
     marks on her back hot and bleeding

Red, so red

        like blood on the goose girl's handkerchief
although her own mother doesn't care
and her own mother is gone forever

                (O, poor child, poor child, poor child.)

A firefly caught in a Mason jar
by a cruel schoolboy.

Evelyn brushes the stubble now grown in on her head,
one hundred times for good luck,
one hundred times to make her forget,
like a hundred years in the tower of a castle
she cannot escape from

She holds the wig against her naked body
stroking it as if it were a cat,
or something else warm to love

She knows no one would believe her
        Her word against his money

                (O, Evelyn, this is a story as old as time,
                that old horned goat of Hades wrought
                          this constant coming.)

Evelyn As Escapee

Harry buys you
        fur, and perfume, and fabric.

He lets you out, sure you will speak
nothing to this world.

                Persephone, meet Philomela.

When he tells you to get up and leave,
        you follow.
When he tells you you will grow to love
        him, you nod.

Visiting an estate in Versailles,
you see New Yorkers you know.
        and you try to keep silent
                      (after all they know Stanny)
and what would they think of you

silence silence silence silence

There is no mother
There is no father
There is no huntsman
to rescue you,
only you rubbing
your shorn head over and over in the mirror

Wake up, sleeping butterfly

        After all, they know Stanny
        After all, they know Harry—

and before your face wets with tears,
the whispered words tumble out

all over the bearskin rug.

They buy you a ticket home.

      Persephone comes up from the underworld
            blinking
                        in a hesitant embrace
          of all that light

      three thousand orange lanterns
                flash
                        light

Demeter's a haunted ship.

                Your mother—
                oh, how cold your mother is—
                she never really acknowledges you again.
                No longer her bébé.

Standing there, you look out at the harbor,
the span of the gray Atlantic

You look at the city skyline
New York, New Land, New Garden

Le bébé, your delicate feet go down
the dock, and you step back into

no garden of Eden
but a green spot on an island
in the middle of nowhere.

Portraits of Evelyn Nesbit,
Adrift, 1904-1905

Evelyn As Persephone: Out of the Underworld

The autumn sunrise lights up the city.
It glows like a pink poppy
in a golden windswept space—

                pink and open, like the flesh
                of a split pomegranate.

O, Persephone, your time
in this daylit world is short
for Hades calls again

(and Demeter's protection
is no where to be found.)

❦

Morpheus might let you dream,
        Sleeping Butterfly

    In the flash
                        lights

of three thousand Chinese lanterns
that glow like chrysanthemums in the park.

❦

Harry's fellow, Longfellow, missed you
on the dock when you disembarked
                How was he oblivious
to that famous head of hair,
                that mouth—

                    O, Evelyn, perhaps you wilted
                    like a flower—lily, poppy,
                                            chrysanthemum.

         Or did you fool him
with a wig? What pose did you make
what costume did you take? Did he
         call you *seducer, siren*
                    snake.

❧

The lights of New York
dazzle you,
blind you
you wonder why you ever
loved this city. It makes you dizzy
in its October evening; orange
and red like fire. It gapes
before you like the mouth of a cave

like the mouth of a bearskin rug
ready to swallow you whole

    All the better to eat you with, my dear.

And the mouth wide open with all those teeth
and inside is blackness

Evelyn As Reflection

Evelyn smiles in the mirror,
at all her gorgeous
straight white teeth
her red lips, her dark hair

                      (now grown back
                      now curling from her head)

all of her glowing again
like a flowering question mark.

Crossing Broadway,
Evelyn thinks of the stage
      where she could pose
             (wild rose)
      where she could hide
             (when the tommies got rotten)

but this time, the doctor warns her not to
                      —Listen to the nice man, Evelyn

She is tired of listening to all
these men who only have her
best interests at heart.

She wonders how many wolves
are in the audience, how they might sniff
her perfumed body

      who is the fairest of them all?
      who is the most tender?

Evelyn As Snow White

After avoiding him, she sees
Stanny on the street

When he calls later, he tells her it is life
and death

and she thinks, funny, I have already died

          but she thinks of her mother
          how she wishes she could kiss her cheek
          how she wishes she could feel her hand
          against her head, stroking her hair,
          in a way she never actually did

and she tells Stanny,
              —Yes, come to me,
              but none of that funny business.

He arrives,
        (oh, kind father, he looks the same)
bearing her mother's concern

and a pair of tiny seedlike pearls,
which he insists she put in her ears.

And he says

            —I've come to talk about Harry Kendall Thaw.
He wonders aloud how she could've fallen—
         Really, Kittens?
        —Everybody knows he's a dope fiend
        and certifiably insane.

    Except no one ever told her.

> *And so, the King knew and said nothing*
> *when the stepmother fed Snow White*
> *the apple, when the huntsman*
> *took her into the woods, knife unsheathed.*
> *He did nothing when she was bought*
> *from a casket and taken to a castle.*

When he tries to kiss her, she turns her cheek.
He tells her that her mama agrees   with him.

      —Go with the nice man, Evelyn.

If Demeter joins forces with Hades, Persephone is left
in perpetual darkness, bloody seeds in hand.

Where was the King when the red apple was placed
in his daughter's hand?

                  (poison is poison is poison)

Evelyn As Automata

Whirl a girl
whirlagig
                spun sugar
whirly girly
                get a part
                (a throwaway in *The Girl from Dixie*)

Bat your eyes,
thank your Stanny
        white fox furs keep you warm

                —Be a good girl, Evelyn
                —Say he's a nice man, Evelyn

Whirl, girl
whirlagig
whirly girly
hurdy gurdy

                all those toy ballerinas
                in the window of FAO Schwartz

                he likes to watch

how they swing up in the air,
against the backdrop of parasols and red velvet.

And you cannot forget how many
shredded moons there are.

Evelyn As Alice

Kisses cannot help you sleep or forget
and you are tired of remembering to forget

Stanny finds a doctor who gives you powders
that taste like apples

            and down the rabbit hole you go

    Dreaming as the days go by,
    Dreaming as the summers die

When you dream
           you dream of Harry
(before the castle)
           in Paris, city of light
(before mad hatter,
mad Harry)

    where everything tasted
    like chocolate and bread
        (so Boofuls)

    Ever drifting down the stream—
    Lingering in the golden gleam—
    Life, what is it but a dream?

Evelyn As St. Maria Goretti

You open the door on your birthday
to Harry, urgent in the threshold.

    —I've changed, dear Eve, I want to marry you.

He stuffs stemless roses,
white ones,
into your palms.

Ah, these decapitated alms.

    —I'll crush them into any perfume you want.
    I'll transform them into gems. All for you.
    Boofuls, all for you.

On Christmas day, they always sing Ava Maria.
Ava. Eva. Eve. Evelyn.

You close the door.
He carols outside it.

    Remember, Christ our Saviour
    was born on Christmas day
    to save us all from Satan's power
    when we were gone astray.
    O tidings of comfort and joy.

You let the roses drop to the wooden floor,
they reflect in the shine, multiple
severed heads.

Evelyn As Beauty

You are wrapped   in chrysanthemums   in a kimono
        Stanford   bought you   when he arrives
at the theater,   his palm spread over   the star
        (your father   said you were   a flashing star)
on your   dressing room door.   Harry is there, too,
           in the audience, and for a brief and translucent
(read transitory)   moment   you have some power
to choose   Which beast for you, Beauty?   Which
red-white-clawed   spectacle   will dance on
 his hind legs for you?   Every thing   you've ever done
           has been a manacle,   soft as velvet or hard
as porcelain.   How could   you not be pained
         by the cycles of spinning,   the ins and outs.
How could you not   want to veer?   Every
Floradora girl   is totally adorable   to him   but
Harry,   now stripped clean,   says he loves you only
so when Stanny arrives, you send   him away.
Later, the doorman   tells how   White rages   furious
you have gone   to meet   that miserable puny
Pittsburgher.   Step.   Ball.   Change.
They each wait.   Your   Ball   and   Chain.

Evelyn As A Collapsed Flower

At Rector's, when the pain
doubles you over,

you see the world
                    dissolve
to a pinprick darkness coming
forward as a cyclone.

Harry grabs your hand
                        and cradles
you to the floor.

When the doctor recommends
rest and then surgery to remove
all those internal adhesions,
                 Harry grabs
your hand and smoothes
the white sheets.

                     He tells you
how he'll pray for you:

      —My beautiful tainted wild rose.
                    Dress in white
for me, little woman
and forget all
                        that red velvet.

When you wake up, *yes*
      whispering in your ears,

is it because you think you love him
or because he doesn't have a wife he can't leave,

no other girl waiting in the wings?

    Stain in the room,
    stain on the bed,
    pain in your gut,
    pain in your head.

And really what's the harm of saying yes.

Harry gives you something, shoots it in your arm
Doctor's orders, he says

      (poison is poison is poison)

Outside you look at the trees
   the buds of spring
      create a green haze
over everything. Is it necessary to see
things clearly?

If you shut one eye the world is one way,
then the other one, other, one, other.

All your life
   there's been no one and now someone
wants you to make a change.

     You would call your mother if you could,
     but she's away on her honeymoon. She
     didn't even invite you to the wedding.

Traveling by darkness,
     without Demeter's light,
how easy it is to descend.

How ineffectual fathers become.
How absent mothers, brothers, friends.

Is it any wonder when Harry confesses
his weakness, the confusion of the night in the castle

                    the error and how much he loves you
truly and that he'll always put you first

you contrast that with the White
            emptiness   void
and is it really any wonder
when you say:
                        —Yes, I will, yes. Yes.
and later sign the certificate
Mrs. Harry Kendall Thaw.

            (Ashenputtel finds her prince
            the glass shoe to wear, never
            realizing glass pierces flesh)

You get used to the descent
down into the dark
once you've traversed it

once you've forgotten
what daylight is

Portraits of Evelyn Nesbit Thaw,
Pittsburgh 1905

Evelyn As Fashionable Bride

Your bridegroom chooses black for you,
never mind the new fad for white.

The stiff lace frames your face,
highlights the white glow of your skin.

He wears white gloves as if to dust you
off, wipe you clean. You catch your mother's

glance in the mirror. She has come, finally,
and your heartbeat whispers, *truce*.

But you see your reflection in the glass's edge,
tiny, broken. Something about the way

she touches your hair makes you think
of vampires.

❃

On your honeymoon,
in Chicago, Harry insists
on staying at the Hotel Virginia
to remind you (of course)
that you have come full
circle and must always
repent for your sins, snake
charmer.
              Ah, Eve, Evie,
Evelyn, Ave, Ava Maria,
bootiful baby.
                    You can
always hope Lake Michigan
will wash away the past.

    The mermaid gave up her voice
    for a prince who did not love her.

You dress in white
(Harry's request)
not off white
not of White
now that you are fully
Thaw.

He loves you, oh he loves you, and he spins you and he loves you and you and he and yes, oh, yes, and all you ever did was receive a kiss, and gifts, and he never really ever tried to hit you.

When will you realize you are sleeping, Beauty?

Evelyn As Cinderella: In the Palace of the Prince

In the city of ash, Evelyn lives
        in Lyndhurst Manor
with her Prince

where the ivy blots the sunlight.

        Inside is out, outside is in.

The evil stepmother guards the other wing
and the family name. No one can know
who this transformed
              (cinder) girl
 is—except, of course, that everyone knows.

Evelyn wanders
this house, this mausoleum.

She walks its hallways wearing white
(always white)
              like some living ghost
who everyone
              pretends is dead and buried.

Round and round, she traces her path

until a servant warns her to not

to hurt the parquet.

So she winds up the staircase
              staring aimless at empty walls.

She is naturally suspicious

of those who hang draperies over art and say
              novels are immoral.

                              —Great God damn!
                              she shouts once
                              when no one is home;

her voice echoes
up and up
along the banisters
puncturing nothing.

Evelyn As Greeted by the Christian Friends of Mother Thaw

You pray at every meal
You go to church every Sunday.
You find they are all so charitable

    tolerant

But their Bible leaves you
with the taste of salt
in your red mouth.

These are not words for you.

And you know their God
is really the Almighty dollar
and they are extremely rich
and you are extremely poor.

And no one is going to forget that.

All those old biddies looking
at you and they say:

    We do not acknowledge
    your name is Evelyn
    or you were on the penny postcard
    or the stage or in a painting
    in the museum

    but we know
    your polluted   body
        slight upbringing

    we know what you are
    we know what you
    we know

      They wait in the wings
                          like buzzards

so tolerant,

and they say:

      You should pray to release
      yourself.

      You should pray to be
      forgiven.

      You listened to the snake
      who owns the garden.

                You looked Hades in the face
                and loved him, Persephone.

They do not hesitate   to take in the curve
of your dress and expose you

      gold digger
                    seductress
serpent
     temptress of their sons.

We refuse to say your name.

Evelyn As Scheherazade

After your first anniversary, Harry begins
to wake you every night
        again
asking for the same old story
                about Stanford White,
            that depraved monster
and defiler of tender girlhood:

He tells you
        you may never mention
his name
      your stain
             keep it under
the veils.

He's a wolf, Evelyn,
He's a wolf, a menace to society
He is the Beast. You must call him only Beast,
or B.   *Do you understand me?*

B in your bonnet, Harry, get it out.

You do not know Harry spends
thousands to have Stanny followed
by private   detectives to and from his theater.

      Little butterfly,
                violence is waiting
        in the wings.

Evelyn As Mediator

You do not know Harry has a gun / how he spends the small hours / of morning / buffing it / to make it shine / until there is / a loud report / (and another!) / (and another!) / from the backyard / and everyone / in the house / hurries out / to see him on / the lawn, shooting / hard at stones, / bricks / wood / firing at foundations / The curl of his lip / his teeth / pulled back / like an angry animal / He looks like the puppy / kicked by the preacher / a week ago / how you screamed / at that frocked man / his pompous face / his beady eyes / his casual cruelty /you are not / a man / of God / you shouted / your pink cheeks hot / with hatred / you and the puppy / were banished / no one / in the household / spoke to you / for days / no one / could speak / to you / for days / now the butler says / "duck" / and you do / a small white pitcher / shatters off a table / "at least / he's a terrible shot," / he whispers / you can smell / his sweat / and he reminds you / of an actor / of Jack / an actor / this surely must / be a play / or a game / but as in nightmares / you don't know / your lines / or the blocking / as you perform / still,
you rise up / and cross the lawn / to Harry / who looks blank / eyes gone bad / like at Schloss-Katzenstein / you place your hand / on his arm / help him lower / his gun / his eyes / black holes / like eyes of animals / you posed on / poor taxidermied things / his lips are cold / you kiss them anyway / breathe life back / into him / although he does not / deserve it / he shrugs away / walks the expanse / of grass / into the house / the gun hanging / like an exclamation / point by his side / he locks it away / but you know / he is the only one / who has the key.

Evelyn As Bodily Parts

Harry shakes you awake
     at dawn and tells you

he's made an appointment with the dentist,
and all
     the nice pearly covering
of your teeth is to be yanked out

because Stanny had it done
and Harry didn't like it.

      He didn't like it at all.
He won't have one part of you. Not one, he says.

Yank it out,
  throw it away.
     Your past is a cancer
Your past belongs underground.

But all things resurface.
You take satisfaction in the knowledge

※

You take satisfaction
in the knowledge
that despite her efforts,
Mother Thaw can't force
the Pittsburgh
sausage company
to rescind a Christmas
ad using your picture.
You smile at her grimace
at your chin caressing

the soft fur above
the jaw of the beast.

❧

You take satisfaction
at her horror when
she discovers the Carnegie
Art Gallery will display
Eickemeyer's "Little
Butterfly."
You envision
the convulsion,
the fluttering
of her heart,
how she must sit
on her bed, hand
clenched until
her nails
make it bleed,
staring at
the catalog description:
Sultry showgirl
stretched at full-length
on a magnificent
polar bear rug.

Your damaged
mouth determines
you'll never smile
that way again,
but photographs
are bits of eternity,
raising their pretty
heads to bloom
like ghosts.
And everything
undone can
be redone.

Harry makes you, his boofuls, pose
for him—   head through the sheet,

hair pulled taut,   pinned to the fabric
and he does not ask
                    the photographer
to simulate blood with red paint,

            but you can imagine
         your stained head
                    Harry sniffs the air like an animal

and you must close her eyes
                        or sigh
                  or part your lips in false ecstasy

or act as if you are dead,

one—all seven—of Bluebeard's wives

It's all part of the game
you must wait out,

You take satisfaction
in the knowledge
that your body
is still there
under a white
sheet.

Portraits of Evelyn Nesbit Thaw,
New York, June 1906

Evelyn As Tourist Of Her Own Past

Harry says, Let's go abroad again,
and Evelyn thinks, alright.
                                  Maybe this time it'll be alright
They'll stay in New York this time,

where she can imagine again
                     the fairyland of the park,
how Stanford's lights hung like oranges
from the trees, fruit in the dark
                     all those years ago

before she knew him.

       Flash
             light

     the city dazzles even as the heat oppresses
     and the sultry air pushes haze over the trees,

shining like fruit in the dark, before she knew
what it was to be plucked.

       Flash
             light

Apparitions float from the crowd as she walks
        through the city at evening

Floradora girls.   Beckwith smelling
of linseed oil. Käsebier. Eickemeyer.   Jack

Jack, oh, Jack, how he loved her and he spun her and he loved her and
yes, oh, yes, she wanted to say yes and she stayed up way past when she
should to stare at those poor shredded moons

       fallen petals   broken pomegranate

Startled, she sees her own face looking out
        from a poster underneath
the subway stairwell
            half hidden in darkness.

She notes she had pretty eyes   once
before they were hollowed out.

Evelyn As Life and Death

You spin through the door of Sherry's
to meet Harry, sitting with
    Tommy McCaleb
      and Truxton Beale,

who killed a man in California,
and was exonerated because a man
   has the right to punish,
       even kill another
         who has dishonored
  his wife or sister.
This fact Harry won't let anyone forget—

Privately, you are glad Harry has left his gun at home.

He is drunk and the bartender is trying to convince
him   not to order more gin
so you all move out again   into the night.

Truxton on one side of Harry, Tommy on the other,
    arm in arm,
the three sing a popular song
   into the moist oppressive air:

> *Why are you so sad?*
> *Come see my Dad,*
> *the little maiden cried.*
> *Long, long ago, he loved me so.*
> *Sadly, the women sighed.*

The heat makes the iron of the city glimmer, appear
as if it's breathing, a sleeping behemoth.

Everyone settles at the Café Martin.

    You think of Rector's, the spun sugar
        pulled and twisted
    by daddies and mothers and lovers
    and you're not even twenty-two

The past walks in, like out of a dream
Stanny with his son.
        Warmth drops
           from you
like a stone.

You turn quickly
but Harry is only staring deep
      into his glass. Four of five litter
        the table, twinkle   in the light
      of the chandeliers and the mirrors

    where you are reflected,
        over and over and over and over,
your small red mouth is an "o."

You know you should hate the Beast,
    the man who tainted you
        left you only pure
           for this dangerous fool
who only wants to wrench you apart.

Oh, why can you not?
    You sigh, relieved, when he moves
        out of view.

Still, you've been well trained by your captor
    and jot a note, pass it over—*The Beast*
        was here but left—

Harry nods calmly, asks if you're all right.

Months later, you wonder
                if Stanny had seen you,
and sensed the danger of his fate,

or pitied you your escort,
           who paced, sweating in his black suit,
straw boater hiding his eyes,

           as he downed one gin and tonic
after another, *to beat*
the heat, he kept repeating
         but he was zig
                  zagging around the room

              —and you—

your gown as white
                  as snow,
            your lips as red
as velvet under a hat swathed in black
gauze,

         were you his lovely Galatea,
once created out of champagne
foam and light?

         Did he worry once again
his treasure was anchored
by the heavy weight
           of that puny playboy,
you played out and bored.

              Did he vow in that moment
         across the room
as it glittered,
              to rescue you again?

      Or at the end, did he see you

                    as the angel of death,
floating like a dark cloud
            through the theater
                        of his life.

When he got up to leave were you
            a snake in his garden
                        or the kind of flower
                                    that blooms
            again and again?

What were his last thoughts of you
            as your eyes met
                        before he spun out the door

into blackness and city light.

Evelyn As One of Millions

Riding in the lift again
to the garden theater
                at Madison Square

(after years away)

              staring into the orange
glow of lights on a string

Evelyn thinks

           of the way fireflies can light
                    up the water, diving

She never dreamed of playing Titania,
      but here in this enchanted night
              she feels as if she could.

She remember how people loved her
           once for her yellow hair,
               or red, or black,
depending on the wig she wore when the lights
came up

      Flash
             Light

She realizes always,   oh, always
there will be a new girl—
             a new model—not her
—to make everyone happy.

In the heat, Evelyn shivers
as the first notes of "I Could Love
a Million Girls" sound.

Evelyn As Lost Child

Harry's face / is round / and flushed / pink / like a pig's / he jitters / in his seat / jumps up / and leaves /paces behind / the tables / You understand / the play / is so bad / no one can / sit still / You fan / yourself / in the heat / companions / whisper / do you want / to leave / Your head / pounds / you nod / but Harry's / chair is empty / He prowls / like a caged / tiger / eyes wide / You wonder / how your mother / could ever / have called / him a good / man / Stanny sits / in his seat / a jolly king / you want / to go / to him / slip / into his lap / have him / cradle you / tell you / this is only / a bad story / it's time / to come / home / he didn't / do it / mean it / all the things / he did to you / just because / you agreed / at fifteen / to go up / in a swing / you close / your eyes / the blackness / behind / your eyelids / a relief / a nothingness / you can pour / yourself into / Harry returns / you get up / mechanically / like some sweet / little automata / Stanny once bought / you so you'd settle / into your seat / on the swing

Evelyn As Witness

You head toward the lift but
turn back

to see Harry behind you,
       his eyes look like a stuffed bear's,
             unblinking—
he stops   swings

and it is almost in slow motion,

       how he raises his arm
       how he points the gun at Stanny's head
       how there is no way for you
           to fly from here to there

Then, the loud report   a second   a third

       like that day on the lawn
       like the preacher and the yelp of the dog

and now people are screaming and crying

Red is now splattered on his white cuffs

He is now sliding from the table,
He is now slumping forward
    and now he is falling to the floor,
his blood now pooling.

       The white table cloth pulled down with his dead body

      Flash
        light

Harry comes to you pale faced, splattered
with Stanny's blood and kisses your cold lips.

        Flash
              light

The lights keep blinking.

        —My God, Harry, what did you do!
        What did you do?
        —It's all right dear, I probably saved your life.
        I've killed your Beast, my Boofuls.

It could've be a fairy tale, a dream, that swung

        hanging, a broken rope

how did it blacken, how did it blacken, how did it blacken,
how did it blacken to nightmare?

Evelyn As Out of Body Experience

She's gone to another world,
      as the stage lights flicker
She wants to cry:

     Look what he did to me. *This* nice man.
     That nice man.

  All the nice men and their prey.
      Wolves. Swine. Mad men.

This man
    brainless on the floor of all he created.

The photographers come with their cameras

    Flash
      light

and the reporters with their cameras

    Flash
      light

     Nice men. Nice men.
Everyone with their lens.

This is a different kind of gaze.
     —Look, look at me! No, me! Me! Here!

The papers say there is invariably "a woman in the case."
The papers say the woman is guilty,
    men will do anything in her name.

     Evelyn remembers their names for her:
     Kittens, boofuls, angel, goddess,
     virgin, le bébé, Evie, Eva, Eve
     temptress, snake

Evelyn As The Center of a Broken Pomegranate

The blackness of the last blood spilling,
the black curtains of the night coming down.

Stanny's blood as red as the velvet swing
as red as the tiger's tongue, his skin
laid flat in the room of his creation.

Beyond the teeth,
a mouth as black as the barrel of a gun
blasting through—

Stanny slumped forward,
blood spilling from him,
red as apples.

        Three thousand lights
        in the trees of the Garden dim.

So much dark blood,
        it's no longer red
            but maroon,
like the center
        of a broken pomegranate.
You are
    the center
        of a broken pomegranate.

        Persephone,
        in your white robe,
        holding your narcissus.

The white petals of you flayed open—
        Pinned in a room, pinned on a bed.

The white table cloth pulled down with his dead body

    Flash
             light

And there's a pain and there's nothing
     except the howling dark.

Evelyn As Elegy

It's complicated
                the way you gaze out
half-inviting us in:

girls like you,
who've been labeled

Kittens, boofuls, angel, goddess,
virgin, le bébé, Ava, Evie, Eve
temptress, snake

Could I have warned you how
poison is poison is poison

See how the white pitcher will be shattered
See how the blood will be spilled
See how the light will be broken

I wish I could've given you
after the solstice, on this day, midsummer
                when the sun stands still
                            and the light rises
                      flashing
a way to be a new Persephone,
a girl with a girlhood,
        a girl still squinting in the field
                  a girl who could pick the golden flowers
                and weave them into her own hair.

I wish I could've offered you protection
I wish that old horned goat, Hades, had never come.

Evelyn, may you lie back and rest your weary head
Evelyn, you poor motherless child,

may everything done be undone.

Notes

The poems incorporate quotes from Lewis Carroll's *Alice's Adventures in Wonderland*, The Lord's Prayer, "Ava Maria," "God Rest Ye Merry Gentleman," and the 1905 song "Daddy's Little Girl." The fairy tales referenced are based on translations in Maria Tatar's *The Annotated Classic Fairy Tales*.

Historical information on Evelyn Nesbit and the White-Thaw murder case comes from *American Eve* by Paula Uruburu and the memoirs of Evelyn Nesbit as well as newspaper accounts of the period.

Information was gathered from the actual photographs and portraits listed in "Evelyn As Exhibition."

"Evelyn As Little Red with Velvet Swing" was originally published as "Little Red Velvet" in *LUNCH Review*, 2016. I am indebted to D. Gilson for all his help and support.

"Evelyn As Quivering Pink Poppy" was published in *Future Fossil Flora*, 2017.

The author wishes to express her infinite gratitude to: Marc Estrin and Donna Bister, for taking a chance on this manuscript and to Michael Cocchiarale for his support and for guiding her to Fomite Press. To my fellow writers, Julie Babcock, D. Gilson, Tyler Heath, Matt Hart, Billy Longino, Jen McClanaghan, Tanner O'Neal, Dan Paul, and Michael Manley, words cannot express my thanks for inspiring, reading and/or editing this manuscript—sometimes more than once. Thanks to John Urban for his amazing photos and enduring friendship. A special thanks to the *Gingerbread House Literary Magazine* staff (Emily, James, Joy, Lauren, Mary, & Tennessee) for being amazing, as well as to my supportive colleagues and friends: Alison Baker, Jenae & Matthew Batt, Andrew Brininstool, Josh Hines, Lisa Fountain, Michael Martin, Dylan & LaShanda Parkhurst, Matt Ramsey, Chris & Jessie Sams, and Michael Sheehan & Mary Woo. To Dana, Joyce, and Jeana, for knowing how to lift someone up. To poet and friend Brett Gaffney, for always being there to transform my writing and my mood and whose expert revisions made this book possible. To the Butterworths, and my extended McDermott family, your support has been endless and always kind, and to John & Audrey, none of this would be worth anything without you. Forever & always, you are my happy ending.

About the author

Photo: John Urban

Christine Butterworth-McDermott is the author of *Tales on Tales: Sestinas* (2010), *Woods & Water, Wolves & Women* (2012), as well as the founder and co-editor of the online journal, *Gingerbread House Literary Magazine*. Another chapbook, *All Breathing Heartbreak* (Dancing Girl Press) is forthcoming.

Fomite

About Fomite

A fomite is a medium capable of transmitting infectious organisms from one individual to another.

"The activity of art is based on the capacity of people to be infected by the feelings of others." Tolstoy, *What Is Art?*

Writing a review on Amazon, Good Reads, Shelfari, Library Thing or other social media sites for readers will help the progress of independent publishing. To submit a review, go to the book page on any of the sites and follow the links for reviews. Books from independent presses rely on reader to reader communications.

For more information or to order any of our books, visit
http://www.fomitepress.com/FOMITE/Our_Books.html

More Titles from Fomite...

Novels
Joshua Amses — *During This, Our Nadir*
Joshua Amses — *Ghatsr*
Joshua Amses — *Raven or Crow*
Joshua Amses — *The Moment Before an Injury*
Jaysinh Birjepatel — *Nothing Beside Remains*
Jaysinh Birjepatel — *The Good Muslim of Jackson Heights*
David Brizer — *Victor Rand*
Paula Closson Buck — *Summer on the Cold War Planet*
Dan Chodorkoff — *Loisaida*
David Adams Cleveland — *Time's Betrayal*
Jaimee Wriston Colbert — *Vanishing Acts*
Roger Coleman — *Skywreck Afternoons*
Marc Estrin — *Hyde*
Marc Estrin — *Kafka's Roach*
Marc Estrin — *Speckled Vanities*
Zdravka Evtimova — *In the Town of Joy and Peace*
Zdravka Evtimova — *Sinfonia Bulgarica*
Zdravka Evtimova — *You Can Smile on Wednesday*
Peter Fortunato — *Carnevale*
Daniel Forbes — *Derail This Train Wreck*
Greg Guma — *Dons of Time*
Richard Hawley — *The Three Lives of Jonathan Force*
Lamar Herrin — *Father Figure*
Michael Horner — *Damage Control*
Ron Jacobs — *All the Sinners Saints*
Ron Jacobs — *Short Order Frame Up*
Ron Jacobs — *The Co-conspirator's Tale*
Scott Archer Jones — *And Throw Away the Skins*
Scott Archer Jones — *A Rising Tide of People Swept Away*

Fomite

Julie Justicz — *Degrees of Difficulty*
Maggie Kast — *A Free Unsullied Land*
Darrell Kastin — *Shadowboxing with Bukowski*
Coleen Kearon — *#triggerwarning*
Coleen Kearon — *Feminist on Fire*
Jan English Leary — *Thicker Than Blood*
Diane Lefer — *Confessions of a Carnivore*
Rob Lenihan — *Born Speaking Lies*
Douglas Milliken — *Our Shadow's Voice*
Colin Mitchell — *Roadman*
Ilan Mochari — *Zinsky the Obscure*
Peter Nash — *Parsimony*
Peter Nash — *The Perfection of Things*
George Ovitt — *Stillpoint*
George Ovitt — *Tribunal*
Gregory Papadoyiannis — *The Baby Jazz*
Pelham — *The Walking Poor*
Andy Potok — *My Father's Keeper*
Frederick Ramey — *Comes A Time*
Joseph Rathgeber — *Mixedbloods*
Kathryn Roberts — *Companion Plants*
Robert Rosenberg — *Isles of the Blind*
Fred Russell — *Rafi's World*
Ron Savage — *Voyeur in Tangier*
David Schein — *The Adoption*
Lynn Sloan — *Principles of Navigation*
L.E. Smith — *The Consequence of Gesture*
L.E. Smith — *Travers' Inferno*
L.E. Smith — *Untimely RIPped*
Bob Sommer — *A Great Fullness*
Tom Walker — *A Day in the Life*
Susan V. Weiss — *My God, What Have We Done?*
Peter M. Wheelwright — *As It Is On Earth*
Suzie Wizowaty — *The Return of Jason Green*

Poetry
Anna Blackmer — *Hexagrams*
Antonello Borra — *Alfabestiario*
Antonello Borra — *AlphaBetaBestiaro*
Antonello Borra — *Fabbrica delle idee/The Factory of Ideas*
L. Brown — *Loopholes*
Sue D. Burton — *Little Steel*
David Cavanagh — *Cycling in Plato's Cave*
James Connolly — *Picking Up the Bodies*
Greg Delanty — *Loosestrife*
Mason Drukman — *Drawing on Life*
J. C. Ellefson — *Foreign Tales of Exemplum and Woe*

Fomite

Tina Escaja/Mark Eisner — *Caida Libre/Free Fall*
Anna Faktorovich — *Improvisational Arguments*
Barry Goldensohn — *Snake in the Spine, Wolf in the Heart*
Barry Goldensohn — *The Hundred Yard Dash Man*
Barry Goldensohn — *The Listener Aspires to the Condition of Music*
R. L. Green — *When You Remember Deir Yassin*
Gail Holst-Warhaft — *Lucky Country*
Raymond Luczak — *A Babble of Objects*
Kate Magill — *Roadworthy Creature, Roadworthy Craft*
Tony Magistrale — *Entanglements*
Gary Mesick — *General Discharge*
Andreas Nolte — *Mascha: The Poems of Mascha Kaléko*
Sherry Olson — *Four-Way Stop*
Brett Ortler — *Lessons of the Dead*
Aristea Papalexandrou/Philip Ramp — *Μας προσπερνά/It's Overtaking Us*
Janice Miller Potter — *Meanwell*
Janice Miller Potter — *Thoreau's Umbrella*
Philip Ramp — *The Melancholy of a Life as the Joy of Living It Slowly Chills*
Joseph D. Reich — *A Case Study of Werewolves*
Joseph D. Reich — *Connecting the Dots to Shangrila*
Joseph D. Reich — *The Derivation of Cowboys and Indians*
Joseph D. Reich — *The Hole That Runs Through Utopia*
Joseph D. Reich — *The Housing Market*
Kenneth Rosen and Richard Wilson — *Gomorrah*
Fred Rosenblum — *Vietnumb*
David Schein — *My Murder and Other Local News*
Harold Schweizer — *Miriam's Book*
Scott T. Starbuck — *Carbonfish Blues*
Scott T. Starbuck — *Hawk on Wire*
Scott T. Starbuck — *Industrial Oz*
Seth Steinzor — *Among the Lost*
Seth Steinzor — *To Join the Lost*
Susan Thomas — *In the Sadness Museum*
Susan Thomas — *The Empty Notebook Interrogates Itself*
Paolo Valesio/Todd Portnowitz — *La Mezzanotte di Spoleto/Midnight in Spoleto*
Sharon Webster — *Everyone Lives Here*
Tony Whedon — *The Tres Riches Heures*
Tony Whedon — *The Falkland Quartet*
Claire Zoghb — *Dispatches from Everest*

Stories
Jay Boyer — *Flight*
L. M Brown — *Treading the Uneven Road*
Michael Cocchiarale — *Here Is Ware*
Michael Cocchiarale — *Still Time*
Neil Connelly — *In the Wake of Our Vows*
Catherine Zobal Dent — *Unfinished Stories of Girls*
Zdravka Evtimova — *Carts and Other Stories*

Fomite

John Michael Flynn — *Off to the Next Wherever*
Derek Furr — *Semitones*
Derek Furr — *Suite for Three Voices*
Elizabeth Genovise — *Where There Are Two or More*
Andrei Guriuanu — *Body of Work*
Zeke Jarvis — *In A Family Way*
Arya Jenkins — *Blue Songs in an Open Key*
Jan English Leary — *Skating on the Vertical*
Marjorie Maddox — *What She Was Saying*
William Marquess — *Boom-shacka-lacka*
Gary Miller — *Museum of the Americas*
Jennifer Anne Moses — *Visiting Hours*
Martin Ott — *Interrogations*
Christopher Peterson — *Amoebic Simulacra*
Jack Pulaski — *Love's Labours*
Charles Rafferty — *Saturday Night at Magellan's*
Ron Savage — *What We Do For Love*
Fred Skolnik — *Americans and Other Stories*
Lynn Sloan — *This Far Is Not Far Enough*
L.E. Smith — *Views Cost Extra*
Caitlin Hamilton Summie — *To Lay To Rest Our Ghosts*
Susan Thomas — *Among Angelic Orders*
Tom Walker — *Signed Confessions*
Silas Dent Zobal — *The Inconvenience of the Wings*

Odd Birds
William Benton — *Eye Contact: Writing on Art*
Micheal Breiner — *the way none of this happened*
J. C. Ellefson — *Under the Influence: Shouting Out to Walt*
David Ross Gunn — *Cautionary Chronicles*
Andrei Guriuanu and Teknari — *The Darkest City*
Gail Holst-Warhaft — *The Fall of Athens*
Roger Lebovitz — *A Guide to the Western Slopes and the Outlying Area*
Roger Lebovitz — *Twenty-two Instructions for Near Survival*
dug Nap — *Artsy Fartsy*
Delia Bell Robinson — *A Shirtwaist Story*
Peter Schumann — *Belligerent & Not So Belligerent Slogans from the Possibilitarian Arsenal*
Peter Schumann — *Bread & Sentences*
Peter Schumann — *Charlotte Salomon*
Peter Schumann — *Diagonal Man Theory + Praxis, Volumes One and Two*
Peter Schumann — *Faust 3*
Peter Schumann — *Planet Kasper, Volumes One and Two*
Peter Schumann — *We*

Plays
Stephen Goldberg — *Screwed and Other Plays*
Michele Markarian — *Unborn Children of America*

Essays
Robert Sommer — *Losing Francis: Essays on the Wars at Home*

www.ingramcontent.com/pod-product-compliance
Lightning Source LLC
Chambersburg PA
CBHW030120100526
44591CB00009B/475